MARGINAL LAND

Marginal Land

M. R. PEACOCKE

PETERLOO POETS

First published in 1988
by Peterloo Poets
2 Kelly Gardens . Calstock . Cornwall PL18 9SA

ISBN 0 905291 94 8

Printed in Great Britain by
Latimer Trend & Company Ltd, Plymouth

ACKNOWLEDGEMENTS are due to the editors of the following journals and anthologies in whose pages some of these poems first appeared: *London Magazine, Poetry Matters, Poetry Review, Prospice, Midnag* (Arts North) *anthology, Poems '86* and *Poems '88* (Lancaster Literature Festival), *The Green Book, PEN Anthology II, An Enormous Yes: in memoriam Philip Larkin, 1922–1985* (Peterloo Poets), *Times Literary Supplement*.

'Memories of the garden' won 1st prize in the 1987 Green Book poetry competition.

'Found poem: from the notebooks of Leonardo' won 2nd prize in the 1987 Bury Metro Arts poetry competition.

'Three reflections on the Creation of Man' won 4th prize in the 1986 Peterloo Poets (Poems about Paintings) Open Poetry Competition.

'Raeburn: the Reverend Robert Walker skating' was commended in the 1985 National Poetry Competition.

'News from Africa' was one of the prizewinning poems in the 1986 Lancaster Literature Festival poetry competition.

'Broody' was one of the prizewinning poems in the 1988 Lancaster Literature Festival poetry competition.

'The bull' was a shortlisted poem in the 1987 Cheltenham Festival of Literature Poetry Competition.

WITH THE ASSISTANCE OF

SOUTH WEST ARTS

For Gerald, to go on with.

Contents

page

9 The goddess

10 Memories of the garden

11 Pig sonnet

12 At the entrance

13 Eastham Street

14 Found poem: from the notebooks of Leonardo

15 103

16 Final reductions

17 One week

18 Three reflections on the Creation of Man

19 All Souls

20 Railway allotments

21 Arion Ater

22 Mummies

23 News from Africa

24 In a country churchyard

25 In memoriam

26 Bindweed

27 *Love me do*

28 The Holy Places

29 Stopping the diary

30 Points of departure

33 Captain Kitto and little Annie

34 The bull

35 Broody

36 Raeburn: the Reverend Robert Walker skating

37 Soap

38 At Appleby New Fair

39 When the potatoes were almost done

40 The terrible games

41 Putting to rights

42 A love poem of a kind

43 By the way

44 Jack

45 Working late on the wall

46 Poacher

47 In November

48 Mr. Burgess has been commissioned to photograph the garden

49   At Manavgat
50   One
51   Honesty
52   Granny knot
53   A hare
54   Old cirrus beard
55   I like watching the nature programmes

The goddess

We startled each other. She was peering
into a wing mirror, one hand flat
to her lank hair. *Lies*, she said.
Get it adjusted. And I know vou
with your pig Latin and your dog Greek
so none of your excuses. Anyway
on a fixed pension one can't afford
even a three-wheeler. I should have enjoyed
a spin down to Staines. So what,
he's past it. – and cackled abruptly,
left arm crooked against long breasts.
The responsibility, she said.
You have no idea of the burden
upon us upon we immortals.
Our times were otherwiser.
  Leaving a river rankness
she passed the bottle bank and the parked cars
and stalked away through willowherb and creeping thistle
with the furious face of a hen.

Memories of the garden

A dark child in summer
dressed in a smock of peartree shadow
leaning her head observes
the vanishing point of afternoon.
Do you hear, Miriam? It is time to go in
and tidy yourself for tea.
Leaves have filled her mouth.

Rose at the Broadwood coaxes dead music.
Madge threads a dune of linen.
Ruth by the cedar tastes her secret name.
The heron has visited, Ma'am
and stolen the goldfish, every one.
The gentlemen are coming by motor.
No more seasons.

My naughty Gyp has killed a lamb
and hidden it under the hives.
The bees are all dying.
Where does this alley lead?
It leads to the counties, the shires,
the continents, the oceans,
the wandering stars.

The sundial's beak has stabbed my bees
my fish and golden lamb.
My sisters have been given in marriage
to men with red whiskers.
They have shot my Gyp.
He is buried at the end of the alley.
Leaves have filled his mouth.

Pig sonnet

The pigs ran tiptoe through their hubbub,
elegant, avid, boistering at the trough,
quarrelled, were neighbourly, could laugh
seizing fresh straw in mouthfuls, squinting up;
until they hung in the barn dumbfounded
in a long arabesque, their stiff lashes
painted with a little blood. There were dishes,
pails, a plastic bag. *Good pigs*, the man said,
holding a bucket of loganberry froth.
They've scraped well. You'll be wanting the blood?
He stood like an artist at the easel,
weight thrown back, appraising. *Good clean pigs*. Death
seemed merely stupefaction: passing, absurd
and, like wax in the ears, remediable.

At the entrance

Came by sporting a nowhere hat,
guitar on his shoulder.
I thought I just ... Hands searching
as though for fee or bribe,
eyes trawling for a shadow that might quake
like candleflame in the darkened hall.

Not in, shaking my human single head.
(Why should imagined loss
hurt like the real thing, and why
his pain become my own?) *Tell her*
I just ... and revved away to the somewhere world,
his back nailed taut in leather.

Eastham Street

Afternoon. The chip shop is closing.
Opening hour now for terrace doors.
Wedges of shadow hold ajar
the terracotta, the flaking brown,
ginger and glossy beige.
Hopscotch pavements beam.

This is the old women's time.
Belayed on cords of fraying breath
they rock in broad shoes to the top of the street
to settle on benches, screaming
like harbour gulls. *Forgot yer pinny, Doris!*
One wears a comfortable hat.

Lightly the northwest wind brooms aside
trash of clouds and words.
Propped on a taffrail of houses
the old women cruise till tea
on salt unvisited blues and greens
of the distant bay.

Found poem: from the notebooks of Leonardo*

Canvas   stone   colours   brushes   palette   sponge.
Borgonzo began and was unwilling
and so fortune deserted him.

Cloth from the excise man. Red Spanish leather.
Giuliano da Maria the physician
had a steward without hands.

Friday morning one florin to Salai
for expenses: he had 3 soldi left.
For bread   wine   eggs   mushrooms   fruit   bran.

One may make of wood thin grained boards
which will seem like camlets and watered silks.
Two dark purple dusters for Salai.

Tuesday you will buy the wine for the morning.
Sawdust of the spindle tree and isinglass
and nuts of cherries and shells of snails.

A light hat. Thatch from the ruined houses.
The mirror of Rosso, to watch him make it.
Sulphur and pitch, sulphur and lead.

The reconciler of the flow and ebb of the sea.
Parsley   mint   wild thyme   burnt bread   vinegar   salt.
To make arrangements for my garden.
Where is Valentino?

*Translated by Edward MacCurdy

She used to talk of Adelaide Street, Albert Street,
and beef fourpence a pound,
of Fred in a poppy coat,
Flo who sang and went for a nurse,
Miss Foster driving a governess cart.
Once, the lad from the sawmill ran
barefoot through Adelaide Street and past the school and down
to the Scotch doctor's house
to have him stitch his cheek back on,
the raw piece in his hand.

She used to remember clothes set out
to last the week, two piles on the one bed:
strings buttons petticoat flounces banged flat;
four piles on two,
stiff woollen shirts, jackets cleaned with spirit.
Where could the rest have slept, each dull Sunday afternoon
counted one by one?
William, Ernest, Maud, Joe,
in Hopes of the Resurrection
under mown chapel grass laid singly side by side.

The past is frayed away;
present, a worn glove. Time's lost all tense
but waiting. Blueblind eyes watch eagerly
till nodding and smiling at the door
Flo who sings as pure as Patti,
Miss Foster hitching her skirt
to thump her boots on the coir mat,
the merry boys, and Fred home from the war
crowd in straight off Adelaide Street, Albert Street
where the motorway begins.

Final reductions

What will become of these, the drab, the harsh,
the sour-coloured, garish,
of sad cloth crudely gathered,
raw-hemmed with hanging thread,
fastened with dull huge buttons, heavy-collared,
drooping on corner racks, each with its affidavit
struck through in red;
the ones twitched over daily
by desultory hands, docketed, cased
in greying flesh finally reduced,
shuffling in rooms and corridors
where a whole summer day
fits a white teacup handed out at three?

One week

The days of this house are unwarmed:
seven empty rooms.
Outside, the weathers come and go,
observed neighbours:

> a zinc sky sifting rain
> a wind belabouring trees
> a sun in pinchbeck.

There is Oneday Twoday etcetera.
Nobody comes.
We will clean the cold spaces.
We will scour scrub straighten burn
check that the mirrors are empty
lock up.
On Sevenday, weep.

Three reflections on the Creation of Man

(Michelangelo: panel in the Sistine Chapel)

In the beginning, Adam, warm as new milk,
drowsing on the pomegranate crust of the world
his eyes filled with the colour of distance
>   and already there will be primroses in the combe of his back
>   a weasel questing for eggs
>   a blackbird after berries
>   an adder coiled in the eye of the sun.

In the beginning, the Ancient of Days
robed in a whirling conch of departure
with flamen and hierophant and the cry of cherubim
>   and already he has caused the pallid sky
>   to flood between his finger and Adam's; separation
>   echoes interminably from hand to hand.

In the beginning, under God's rooted arm
Eve like a foxcub, quick for danger and delight.
She has tasted the blood of loss and making
>   and already she trusts no one
>   gives nobody her hand
>   knowing that stories contradict
>   and apples will not keep.

All Souls

Blinds drawn down till April.
Standpipe lagged. Wind tipping
the lees from a paper cup.
Horizon coldly inked. Daymoon frailer
than broken bread.

Tomorrow comes All Souls.
The air testing my coat
the sea sliding in channels
to left and right intent as a collie
warn me to leave.

From this disfigured sand
the last are gone to fold.
The page is printed. Slowly
a wordless grey absolving tide rubs out
all wounds and spoils.

Railway allotments

Near blackened alcoves
just where the sun's cut off
and peers through grilles
at fantasies of sooted brick
(English bond meticulously ordered),
clear of the frassy tunnels
where diesels bore and cough
and the electric engines sigh,
outside Birmingham Exeter Sheffield Stoke
retired men nurtured
upon implacable texts gingerly unbend
above their linear gardens bordered
with creosoted sleepers,
and shrug their coats and stand
watching for the express to saunter through.

Then turning to their loves,
their strips of peas crosshatched,
Maris Piper stitched in knots of green
along the steady rows, they contemplate
their manuscripts of common prayer
made brilliant with shallots; intercede
that Autumn King and Greyhound may mature,
each white Musselburgh
stand in its paper collar
like a marble pillar, ruby red Detroit
grow thick and firm,
the Stuttgart Giants raised from seed
be slender in the neck and touched
with gold, while the three twenty runs to time
each leisured afternoon.

Arion Ater

I never see you arrive.
When clouds hang sodden
beyond the power of wind to move
you visit the underlight.

Imperceptibly and certain
as growth of leaves and grasses
you become present
browsing a drenched continent

as glossy as fish
and grandly mantled, blacker
than Angus bulls. Only your name
irritates like salt in cuts.

Yet when I consider, I see
it is all that you need: slug.
No name at all, but a code
for your secrecy.

Your ridged and gleaming hide: glus.
Your intent slow coupling: lusg.
Your rasping and swallowing: guls.
Sulg: your stealthy peace.

Mummies

Mummies are nice.
They tell you what you feel and brush the lies
like maggots from your eyes.

Under their feathers snug and warm
they suckle ghosts that keep your soul from harm
wherever you may roam.

They teach you from the start
to keep an eye on your deceitful heart
ready to scald the tainted part.

Even from the grave
they call cooee, manage a wave
that says, Now you're a Mummy too, be brave,
we know you know the right way to behave.

News from Africa

One April morning it was there
threading new sunlight between rafters.
Today the cat offers it indifferently,
folded like a paper dart.

Its back is ruffled indigo,
its throat desert colour. One eye gleams
in a head twiddled loose. Tail and beak
are strokes of a cancelling pen.

On an inside page, photographs
from Tigre province: parched skins tattooed
with indigo, and children's heads that dangle
over the arms of old men.

In a country churchyard

Two groups, a post and rails between
Dividing mown from rougher green.
This side a modest huddle stands
Concealing griefs with folded hands
As plastic turf keeps eyes away
From indiscreetly naked clay.
The parson with an anxious look
Holds down his surplice with his book
And vouches for the God of Love,
While on the other side there shove,
To take what pleasure life allows,
Eleven cumbrous Friesian cows
That belch and stamp and groan and wag
Their ears each with its yellow tag
And jostle for a better sight
Of humans, likewise black and white,
Who fix their gaze on trampled grass
And one small box of pine and brass.

    Creator God, be pleased to give
The gift of laughter while we live,
And when we die pray then explain
The purpose of our cruder pain.

In memoriam

and some there be which have no memorial
such as Miss Lattimer whose son was no good
and whose hope was in the bingo caller.

Heavy Miss Lattimer with the white hand
pigmented in patches, whose large pale eyes
moistened while reading DOG THROWN FROM HIGH
  WINDOW,

Sally of the swollen knees, jumble sailor
intrepid among charity's flotsam,
what kind of memorial would you have wished?

Your joy was a little bottle of Chypre,
a plastic rose, a tabby cat that has gone
to another place, they say a better

like you, Sally, whom I forget for months
at a time; till arbitrary things – a mop,
a sweet chemist's counter stink – present you
solid as a monument; and then I know
that your name liveth until it's my turn.

Bindweed

You'll not get rid of em, said the retired man
knocking mud from a boot.
No clearing those. Worse than twitch, for my money.
When the cathedral was bombed, twenty foot down
in the craters I saw em, fresh bits of root.
And where d'you suppose that come from?
There since they dug the crypt, that's what I say.
Twenty foot down, biding their time.

These I recognise. Hoed out, they snap
without resistance: sepulchred deep in clay
and swelling unacknowledged through a lifetime's
airless civilities, unobtrusive,
surreptitiously alive,
the hatreds ripening under day,
biding their time; every blanched scrap
a strangler proffering light bruisable blooms.

"Love me do"

(Samantha, died of a brain tumour aged 17)

Cheap music dares conviction,
lays it on the line
in spite of disbelief,
belts out *I'll never leave you,*
I'll always be true.
The raw emotion
bears a false rhyme or two,
banality of pain and grief,
cos you don't know the journey
I got to go.

Sam with a flowered scarf
over her pitted skull
sang *Love me tomorrow*
brashly like a wren,
trusting the thumbed chords
and style she followed
would see her through.

Hope vamped till ready.
Then on florists' cards
another set of phrases
as trite and wired with pain
but with no voice to shock them into life,
no pulse of luck and courage:
Till we meet again.
Forever in our hearts.
Always.

The Holy Places

(Found poem: from a conversation on the road to Lindisfarne.)

You won't get across to Lindisfarne,
not tonight you won't. Tide's coming in.

> *Our Arthur died when he were nearly ten.*
> *That's when I started going to the Holy Places.*
> *Being a railway man I get free passes.*
> *Put me bike and stuff in the luggage van.*
> *I travel light. Canvas bags I got.*
> *That Marj were a bugger she were, smoked in bed*
> *so I left her, couldn't stand the way she cried*
> *behind her specs. Rome I've seen, the lot.*
> *Walsingham. Moscow with me Union card.*
> *That were alright. Assisi. Been to Lourdes.*
> *I'm not religious, mind. I've touched the Pope.*
> *That place in Ireland, that were bloody good,*
> *everyone on their knees and drinking hard.*
> *Get to that Lindisfarne tonight I hope.*

Not till tomorrow. Tide'll soon be in.
> *Oh – but tomorrow I've got to catch me train.*

Stopping the diary

So, they have moved you to a harder bed
And changed the sheets and put the flowers away.
Somebody crisp tipped the venetian blind
Abolishing the bleak December day
And stood aside to let the trolley through.
The same thick pillow props a different head.
Would you have been surprised, or would you mind
(As if you're there to mind!) hearing your name
Pronounced tonight to folk you never knew
In the respectful tone of public grief
Used for assured, uncontroversial fame?
      Would it have made you laugh?

I wonder, sitting by a fire that blurts
And grumbles and grows reticent, where you are.
The muddied fields are empty, the long coats
Have stolen home for comfort, drink, a prayer;
While others, I suppose, disguising haste,
Eager to take a scalpel to your hurts,
Are hurrying with credentials, files, notes,
To catalogue ironies and rhymes; confirm
Oldfashioned skills are in; declare what waste
It was, that puzzling unproductive blank
Of your last years; publish, and make a claim
      On quadrangle and bank.

That friendly, gloomy face I can't recall
Except from photos; have no anecdote
About some chance encounter in the stacks,
No inside information; cannot quote
More than a phrase or two. The same hacked tranche
Of time is all we shared, not even Hull
Or cold northeastern valleys scabbed with brick.
Yet since you've snuffed it, how the dark creeps in.
You never took a stand or tried to staunch
The draining out of hope, or begged a cure.
Odd how wry private truths of one who's gone
      Disturb and reassure.

Points of departure

1. GOING AWAY
I'll see you off.
Your kiss is a little shove
though you're the one leaving.

There's much not said.
What's spoken sounds absurd
like speeches at a wedding.

Wave to the person
you thought you'd seen.
I'll look up and smile: we're learning.

With practice
we'll get the knack of loss.
What's heaviest is need of blessing.

2. TOWARDS A RITE OF PASSAGE
What ceremony can we use?
We grow smaller and smaller. Your voice
is a spider filament, dust wand,
pattern traced in air.
I still call out at times, but the trouble
stays the same, I can't lift my head,
so heavy with unassimilated grammars.
Wait, I will show you the dance of the dead,
distant, tiny, done without partners.

Do you see how the leaves turn
rib side up? That means rain.
Soon you will reach desired ground.
Somebody's waving down there
by the homely roof and growing audible.
I am bending down, laying a flat stone
on this hearth, in case. The breeze
is feathering ash in no clear direction
and flicking it into my mouth and eyes.

3. THE TEACHING OF RAIN

Rain is belabouring me
with small blows. The drops assemble
kissing like mercury
on my darkened sleeve. Inside,
my warmth is shrinking to a star.
Here is a drop split off.
They say he who hesitates
is lost. If I were you, drop, I'd
hesitate. It wriggles
to a new place. So I shift
and follow the spent cloud which trails
eastward, resembling smoke.

4. KEEPING IN TOUCH

What shall I say if you write kindly
on coloured postcards, asking me how I am?
I'll list some suitable remarks. *Seems an age
since the swallows left. Drops on the gate
were ice this morning. Dogs caught a hare,
a big buck, heavy. I lugged it home
and got blood all down my trousers.* I'll say
*It's foggy, can't see anything. On average
not bad considering the time of year.*
     I could enquire if you'd read about Surtsey
erupting again. That might seem awkward chat,
though, mightn't it? – implying the bulge of fire
through iceblack water. You'd be bound to envisage
eventual colonies of algae; I'd spy a pinman Adam,
orderly, celibate, ripe for marriage, there in good time
to name each creature, already charting an anchorage.
So: *Now I'd better get a move on, it's late.*

5. IN THE MONOCHROME

I will dance without music.
With an antique severity
I say to my arm, It behoves you
to extend; and it extends
in a leaden sleeve. To my legs
I say, Move. They move numbly, numbly
along the valley of bones.
My eyes are ajar. Across them
begin to run grainy occasions:
a nodding branch, a tangle
of mint, grass, gravel, the calyx
of a bruised poppy split with scarlet.

It would be easier to stand in the monochrome than to take on
this red.

This red begins to command me, orders
the jerking of my pulpy heart, strips off
the dirty bandages of grief,
asserts a rhythm in the lung,
forces the spine to get the hang
of hanging on until the will
relinquishes the puppet skull,
and the knack of being,
of being alive, drains back
half laughing half cursing,
and the ordinary hum
and bopadeedap of morning begins.

Captain Kitto and little Annie

Thinking he hears the children, Captain Kitto wakes
and shifts, and smiles; sighs in anticipation;
draws from his navy jacket chinking shells,
and waits; and sleeps again. His seamed cheeks
beneath the visor's curve are stained palm-green.
    Eyes on the canvas bulges, Annie steals
across the lawn's viridian deck, her breath
held like a captive petrel, till she peers
down at his freckled deepseasleeping head.
Under the sky's blue swell the few pale hairs
waver like seaworms. Close, her own head bowed,
she hears with glee the cowrie-clack of ancient teeth.

The bull

Encountering him elsewhere, at a field corner
or under a masking sycamore, nose to his heifer's tail,
I'd have fled slow as in dreams to the safe side,
heart bucking, apprehension needling
the back of my hand.
    Here, leaning over the half-door,
I broke open a bale of sweet leisure, dawdling,
my back in summer, head in cool;
considered him, enjoyed, grew accustomed:
the broad concave forehead,
bulk of neck, mound of shoulder,
darkness weighed against the darkened stall;
constellation; god;
bull that Europa rode, bridling
his splendour with a chain of stars.
                    I turned,
pulled a sheaf of sour grass and chickweed
growing at the barn wall
and offered it. Then I saw his eyes' uncertain stare,
the dulled metal of his nose-ring
and how his tongue was slimed.
He switched his tail, skin trembling
against the insolence of flies. I was ashamed,
knowing my courage rhinestone; his, uncut opal;
my sabbath locked to his servitude,
my freedom rooted in his dung and mire.

Broody

Lifted, she's a sleeper
jostled in the dead time:
puffed, claggy-feathered.

Begins, step and step.
Close, open, stretch.
An old dancer limbering up.

Nibbles a dish of rain.
At each sip raises
her obsidian beak, like praying.

Shudders, curvets
on cramped lizard legs
and flaps, and shrieks. Subsides.

Taps at a grain or two.
Clucks sotto voce. (Was that the way
the tune went?) Stertorously, shits.

Lifted back, she settles
to the twelve eggs like a coracle
gaining still water;
shuffles down, and broods.

Raeburn: the Reverend Robert Walker skating

In a diocese of ice
the Reverend Doctor with exact calves
draws a distinction
between enthusiam and grace;
pursuing a predilection
for metaphor, observes
how by faith's slender keel his course
is safely etched and leaves
on obdurate surfaces the measured trace
of swift judicious action.

O *dulce et decorum*
here in a temperate age
to glide and glide upon the middle ground
doing the will of man. *Le style, c'est l'homme*
and stylishly he threads the needle's eye, bound
by an impeccable blade's edge
to the freezing fulcrum
set between elements. He has construed this passage;
yet other texts, elusive cruxes, haunt in form
of paradox like the harsh wind that makes his cheekbones burn.

It is almost dark.
The hills preach frosty doctrine.
With hands pushed deep in sleeves
he leans for shore and a cold kirk
to exchange this fluent cursive
for rusty print foursquare on a lectern.
Time to tutor a shivering flock
unscholarly and foreign
as men who once on a drowning deck
watched fearfully a barefoot traverse of waves.

Soap

(Jottings from the notebook of Herr A. Leo, who in 1672
sent from Italy to the Lady von Schleinitz a parcel of soap
with a detailed description of use.)

Lady, this alabaster ...
Having in the course of my travels (Peregrinations?)
Heureux qui comme Ulysse –

Take a bason of soft water.
Moistening between the palms of the hands this ... ?
Having but little skill, Madam, to

– such ablutions as the most refined life
must occasionally necessitate, even
in our more frigid northern parts.

Parts! Those parts which Actaeon, greatly daring (?)
When chaste Diana, at her bath surprised ...
Prized. This gift, though poor, yet prized.

Having observed at the Court of Savona
among those beauties most ... Among those hills.
Odorous hills of pearl(!)

Those perfumes most esteemed among Princes.
Arabian princes? Arcadian?
Arcadian shepherdesses!

Those cheeks like unto ...
Washed in the (Laved?) I beseech you,
Madam, favourably to –

If in the common parlance

Your Ladyship's most (etc.)

Soap, Madam. Soap.

At Appleby New Fair

1. LADY LUCK

Grand hair swaggering as rich as malt.
Pink plastic leather this year and butterfly combs
in liquorice colours. Sharp girls buying whelks.
You've a lucky face lady
There's somebody troubled in the back or the legs
but you'll never tell your worries.
Lightfingered nickel charms
charm nickel from a lucky purse.

Strapped wrists, split leather aprons this year
as before Agincourt or Troy. Hot metal dings.
A priestly acrid smoke drifts up. Eight nails stun home.
A stallion hammers tarmac
showing his paces. Tethered under the bruised hedge
unshod, slacking his truncheon out
this skewbald tips a hoof,
troubled in the back or the legs.

2. UNDESIRABLE RESIDENCE

This is the van that Mick sold
and Jack before him: crazed toffee paint,
tyres flab as a worm,
tacking through seasons, making shift
yard by verge by grit by grass
Appleby Gateshead Morpeth Brough Leeds
Sun Lion Grapes.
                    Here in reeking dark
a lean lad pulled the blankets round,
emerging now from the clapped-out pupal husk
the full florid imago: spinnaker belly,
neckerchief, yellow boots; raising a thick fist
to chalk up boldly FOR SAIL.

When the potatoes were almost done

When the potatoes were almost done
the sick man in the corner chair
recollected himself, planted his knees
untypically, and died.

One daughter ran to turn off the gas,
one seized a gingham napkin, dabbing
at furtive spittle on his chin, and one
jostled him, like a passenger
who bursts on to the platform
when the train is minutes gone.

The terrible games

A noise I heard, something like laughter.
I believe they may be celebrating a murder.
Should I wait outside this door till they call my name?
Must I sit in this cupboard for a long time?
Ought I to have guessed the way the cards were stacked?
Need I be funny before passing this parcel on
or swallow the stuff on the tray for fun?

A message has come inviting me
to a party to end all parties where we shall play
one of the terrible games. I don't know the date.
I had better lie down and shut my eyes tight.
If I count to the number that proves correct
will there be prizes? Will someone explain if I fail?
Oranges and lemons, the axe can spell.

Sometimes I stagger, sometimes I spin
deft as a moth or an angel secure on a pin.
The postman knocks; the voices cry How green you are!
You've missed your turn! Blindfold, dumbfold, play by ear,
you're in, you've won, O,U,T, the teams are picked.
Grandmother light me a candle the thief's in my bed.
Who can teach me the rules for playing dead?

Putting to rights

That slate sky should buckle
under the huge decaying moon; the fells,
when the wind flays them, howl.
When the dead speak, the heart
should burst its capsule, shedding griefs
on good ground and stony.
But we go about our business,
measured, like gardeners, putting to rights.

A love poem of a kind

When you take off your glasses and I observe how nakedness
    floods in
I am reminded of worms that cross the road in the rain
devoid of all except an intolerable pinkness of skin.

I remember hospital visits, having to strip and put on
a small split gown.
Don't worry, these minor deaths (they say) are quite routine.

Now that the nights are drawing in, you've more sense than to
    rage,
reserving energy and cunning to bargain with old age
but I notice you glance at me, and guess you're wondering how
    I'll manage.

Love, as the poet said to himself on the beach, let us be true
to one another, because it's the only bearable thing to do,
to trust each other to laugh, you for me and I for you.

By the way

Years ago the train stopped somewhere, waiting
in the wings of a drab town. What the plot was,
where we were going, I don't remember.
It was brick country, flat and undefined.
Sunshine that morning; the sky bluish;
clouds piled at a far edge like old snow.
Round us, a cinder desert where coarse grass
hung on in tufts. People refolded papers,
keeping their elbows close, and stared out
at the last slick of building. Over the fence
corner to corner on the end house but three
in thick dribbling letters: WELCOME HOME GEORGE.

Clocks started again and we moved, stiffly,
qui, qui, towards supposed destinations.
Women picked up magazines: *qui venit*:
wanting to know what happened. *Dictus qui
dictus benedictus* and round the block
in nomine in nomine steps George looking taller
and we know that somehow after all these years
there's a dénouement, everyone's in,
kettle boiling, duffel bag in the hall.
We're moving now, *domini domini domini*
and the dog's running around grinning and crying
in the grief of catharsis because George is back.

Jack

School's out. Who'll be He?
Who'll be the fearful bird
that feeds its young on sailormeat?
Who'll whistle and lap blood?
Who'll press coins in the terror slot
till the wires start screaming,
drive the stampede   play gorgon   loose and bind?

Who will be victim
and write on limestone eight foot thick
Celui qui n'est pas heureux?*
At dusk spying the latch move
panic into the net
drop the key   forget the password   hide
so well he's lost for good?

Jack the dandelion,
casual as bread and cheese,
bird in the hand and cloak of lies,
made a mock of rules;
set dunderheads to slog it out,
eavesdropped   stole eye and tooth
married the princess   picked the wishbone clean.

*cut into the dungeon wall at Loches

Working late on the wall

Working late on the wall.
Colour has fled into the rising moon.
My hands see shapes of stone.
Humped and huge the fell
is a darkening province where the sharp stars beckon
to children still at play. Time to go in.

I stay to set another block
clumsily, and then one more,
grope in the grass for hearting stones. Aware
that all will be to unpick
in critical daylight, still I peer
hopefully bending there.

Hopeful or doubtful: hard to tell.
Stumbling, I drop a stone and strike
an apricot spark, bright as the moon
before it blanched. Where has my light gone?
I stand and listen
for children's voices on a different hill
too far away to hear.

Poacher

Through gulfs of ice the poacher treads
and takes his trick where winter rides.
Through charcoal dusk he draws his knife
and gathers in a freezing sheaf.
Now let the snow fall thick as moss
and under hedgerows feign a peace,
fall fierce and light, disguise the wound,
cover the track of stoat and hound;
while firelight winks below the hills
and shadows stiffen under walls
the poacher cuts a gasping swathe
and makes a posy out of death.

In November

"Ought not these oldest sufferings of ours to be bearing more fruit by now?" (Rilke)

November searches me.
When thrushes sing requiem
in the yellow chapel of elm and lime
and starlings try old texts,
how I long for a steady rhythm,
the sweet iambics of amended life.

To be orderly and convinced!
To have stored a single unblemished fruit!
On the table a basket
of smutted pears; outside,
ladder not stowed away,
secateurs lost and barrow piled
with nameless soft corruptions.

In a house of twigs a child weeping
for the pattern the kaleidoscope
will not give back. Against a stone
dahlias in a jar. In Arden
an old fool particoloured
venting his observasíon
in mangled forms.

Was it always too late?
Seventy times seven, seventy times seven
sang a voice in the fallen garden
but labouring Adam never turned to ask
for a second chance.

Mr. Burgess has been commissioned to photograph the garden

Grandfather's vine: tendrilled, shadowy, potent,
in the perfection of a certain summer
to be recorded for posterity.

Problems of aperture and exposure
perplexing to one more at home with velvet,
a chair with cabriole legs, a palm in a pot.

Hard to do justice to the vine – but the girls!
They were never mentioned. Inverted lilies,
girls with ambivalent eyes. Aperture –

focus – exposure of considered sleeves –
discomfiture occasioned by white dresses!
Merciful discretion of a black cloth!

Mockery of girls in porcelain blouses.
Complicity of shadows. Ripe fruit unpicked.
Monochrome imperfect record of time lost.

At Manavgat

At Manavgat the old man set his foot
in the waterfall on some invisible ledge,
let in his basket and stood, his arm blanched
by pounding yellows. Rags of his hair streamed out;
till, balancing himself back, he grinned and showed us,
in the depth of his frail, a fish.
    I see now: the art is, to endure
the bellow of falling water; to root in;
to be hungry enough.

One

I praise the eyeless simplicities
that befriend us: worm, mite, spore,
that need no voice.
I bless the error
that preserves us world without end
from being immortal,
when one cell
slips from its narrow task to gift us
with the trivial sufficient wound.

Each winter we invent once more
in the image of desired childhood,
freed from the splendour
and folly of procreation, God,
who evades us: voids, divides, dumb
as an amoeba, multiple as the stars,
and hangs himself and dies.
The latest gift is always myrrh;
the latest lodging place an empty tomb.

Honesty

I've picked one roundel one slip
of paper money one membrane
separating nothing from nothing.

It is pale. Its protectors
have shrivelled beyond use. Its seeds
have dislodged and lodged again somewhere.

After the invasive growth
of crude leaf and purplish blossom
one would hardly have expected this

though of course it's picked in sheaves sometimes
to look bright in a dull corner
along with chinese lanterns

and dusty stiff everlasting flowers
poked into a suitable pot.
Who first named you I wonder.

Patience and Prudence Constance and Grace
the sibilant virtues were called
long ago to the kitchen

and the parlour to do their good works.
How is it that you don't share your name
with sisters? You winter out

as thin as the moon which vanishes
(though we hardly notice) and will
(presumably) reappear.

Granny knot

Rabbit comes out here: your working end.
Round the tree — there — back in the hole.
Now take a grip (you see?) and pull!
A perfect bowline. Fisherman's bend
she taught, sheepshank, lark's head,
hitches for boats and horses: all
a tented garden Indian or wasteland
pioneer could need, demonstrated.
Obedient to her milk-thin hand
the length of string was wound,
knotted, unknotted.

Once, in her room, she loosened pin by pin
her faded chestnut hair
and leaning toward the mirror
uncoiled it in a skein
beside her faded neck,
spread it on her shoulder
strand by strand across skin
yellow as tired silk.
Watching, the child drew back,
dismayed to learn of knots that slip and tighten
and will not pull undone.

A hare

Tom killed a hare.
The october-coloured body thrashed.
He shook it, chopped it,
dropped it stretched out long,
laughed with his tongue and watched it where it lay.

It hangs now in the shed,
one rowanberry bead dry in its ear.
Since the kill its shrieks have meshed my brain,
flicking the memory through, slow-motion.
Nothing provokes its still carnelian eye.

Rain has begun
and bracken sprawls at the fell foot,
a dragged moorit pelt.

Note: "Moorit" properly describes the tan colour of some Shetland fleeces.

Old cirrus beard

Old cirrus beard, old thunderhead
enthroned above flat earth, minatory
on a couch of cumulus, decree nisi
thrust at us like a trident: it's no good.
Your laser shows are spectacle, not threat.
Nobody much now takes you at your word.
You've grown just a cloud, a moderate hazard
like drifting fog, to puzzle heads at night.
    We miss you though. Maybe one shouldn't meddle
with antique systems; one can't judge the cost.
It's dull without your vehement right and wrong.
Except ourselves, no one to try to diddle
or try to love; and when the jets scream past,
nothing to fear except the fear of nothing.

I like watching the nature programmes

How the Venus flytrap
clips to upon its lovers, and sundew
treacles the feet of flies; how foxes
move house to inner cities (subject,
naturally, to urban ills); how bears
starve out gestation, snugged where winds
can't zero in, white in white dens: that's what
(specially on Sundays, when we've swallowed
the quick capsule, the bulletin)
we love to view. It takes your mind off things.
Television's wise, adjuring us: Be expert
in the passions of spiders; as for what's current
in the human heart, don't look too close.